Letting Everything
Become Your Teacher

ARRIVING AT YOUR OWN DOOR:
108 Lessons in Mindfulness
(compiled with Hor Tuck Loon)

COMING TO OUR SENSES:
Healing Ourselves and the World Through Mindfulness

THE MINDFUL WAY THROUGH DEPRESSION:
Freeing Yourself from Chronic Unhappiness
(with Mark Williams, John Teasdale, and Zindel Segal)

EVERYDAY BLESSINGS:
The Inner Work of Mindful Parenting
(with Myla Kabat-Zinn)

WHEREVER YOU GO, THERE YOU ARE:
Mindfulness Meditation in Everyday Life

FULL CATASTROPHE LIVING:
*Using the Wisdom of Your Body and Mind
to Face Stress, Pain, and Illness*

Letting Everything Become Your Teacher

100 Lessons in Mindfulness

JON KABAT-ZINN

Excerpts from *Full Catastrophe Living*
Compiled by Hor Tuck Loon and Jon Kabat-Zinn

Delta Trade Paperbacks

Contents

Acknowledgments

This gift would not have come to fruition were it not for the following kindness and openness—

I'm indebted to Jon Kabat-Zinn for his gracious open-heartedness in giving the initial permission to compile the verses which make this book possible. Chee Fun for her precious time in going through the draft of this work in the earlier stage, Becky and George for their continuous feedback, assistance, and sincerity. The many spiritual seekers who have touched my life in many great ways, thus making them my teachers. Most important of all my wife, Lai Fun, who makes her life my lessons in mindfulness and patience to deal with my own shortcomings.

Hor Tuck Loon

Preface

This book was first conceived in 1992 when I had just exited from a month's meditation retreat and was recommended by a friend to read *Full Catastrophe Living* by Jon Kabat-Zinn.

I was instantly enthralled by the depth and clarity of Jon's work on mindfulness in his eight-week program at the Stress Reduction Clinic, University of Massachusetts Medical Center. While going through the book, I highlighted the verses relevant to my own level of practice at that time. I was so inspired I wanted to compile a book then . . . but there it remained—an inspiration!

After more than ten years of mindless deliberation and procrastination, I was again inspired by the verses I had previously highlighted—this time with a different level of understanding knitted to a fresh perspective out of my recent insight meditation practice, where an emphasis on right attitude in the watching mind matters more than what is being watched or experienced—"... how you relate to the sensations you experience makes a big difference in the degree of pain you actually feel and how much you suffer." (Jon Kabat-Zinn)

Though the words are the same as a decade ago, my understanding now differs greatly: there is a deeper sense of clarity and purpose. Whatever level of practice we are at, Jon's articulate style allows each person to resonate with the verses at their own personal level.

I wish to present Jon's work in this collection of verses as a gift to readers to inspire them in their meditation practice, for whether during a retreat or in their daily life, mindfulness practice and life are inseparable.

May this little offering be a guide to those passionate seekers who are in this life seeking within.

Hor Tuck Loon

Introduction

18,000 medical patients and almost thirty years of experience and scientific studies from the Mindfulness-Based Stress Reduction (MBSR) Clinic and Center for Mindfulness at the University of Massachusetts Medical Center have shown us that the cultivation of greater mindfulness through regular systematic formal and informal meditation practice can make a huge difference in the quality of life of people with a wide range of chronic stress disorders, pain conditions, and outright illness, to say nothing of those suffering from the normal wear and tear of the constant and mounting stress that is part and parcel of our everyday lives in this culture of 24/7 connectivity and multitasking. These pressures on our lives make it more and more difficult to find time for being and for moments of *non-doing* that might restore us, body and soul. Such moments, always available to us, but so easily missed, also allow us to remember, pay attention to, and embody what is most important in our lives, rather than getting caught up in the endless stream of what is most demanding or seductive.

This book of excerpts from *Full Catastrophe Living*—the book in which mindfulness meditation, the MBSR program, and the applications of mindfulness to stress, pain, and illness are described in great detail—can give you a doorway into the practice of mindfulness and the rediscovery of what is deepest and best in yourself. Any one, or any number, of these 100 pointers can readily remind you of what you already know in a deep way, that you actually have a choice in every moment: the choice of how to be in wise relationship to this moment, inwardly and outwardly, no matter what is happening. By taking responsibility for your own experience in this way, you are taking a profound and potentially transformative step toward both healing and genuine well-being and happiness, not in some better "future" that may never come, but in the only moment you ever have for living, for breathing, for loving, for being . . . namely this one. You already have this power. It is innate in all of us. All it takes is paying attention, and being kind to yourself; and persevering in remembering that you are alive only in this moment, and now is the only time you ever have for making choices, and that this *now* is always available to you. Every moment is indeed a new beginning.

Since you have only moments to live, why not live them completely, and find out what it might mean to be true more of the time to your own deepest, most authentic nature?

This book was developed by Hor Tuck Loon of Malaysia out of his own passion for mindfulness and a desire to bring it to a wide range of people who are stressed and suffering in various ways. I am greatly indebted to him for both the idea of this book, and for its execution, which includes his own original photographic and graphic artistry, and his own choices in how to emphasize the transformative potential of mindfulness. The product is saturated with his generosity and spaciousness of heart.

Jon Kabat-Zinn
August 2008

Letting Everything
Become Your Teacher

Mindfulness is a lifetime's
journey along a path that
ultimately leads nowhere,
only to who you are.

Self-Motivation 1

In order for meditation practice to take root in your life and flourish, you will have to know why you are practicing. How else will you be able to sustain non-doing in a world where only doing seems to count? What will get you up early in the morning to sit and follow your breathing when everybody else is snug in bed? What will motivate you to practice when the wheels of the doing world are turning, your obligations and responsibilities are beckoning, and a part of you decides or remembers to take some time for "just being"? What will motivate you to bring moment-to-moment awareness into your daily life? What will prevent your practice from losing energy and becoming stale or from petering out altogether after an initial burst of enthusiasm?

Map Versus Journey 2

This book is meant to serve as a map, a guide to you. As you know, a map is not the territory it portrays. In the same way you should not mistake reading this book for the actual journey. That journey you have to live yourself, by cultivating mindfulness in your own life.

3 Personal Vision

To sustain your commitment and keep your meditation practice fresh over a period of months and years, it is important to develop your own personal vision that can guide you in your efforts and remind you at critical times of the value of charting such an unusual course in your life. There may be times when your vision will be the only support you will have in keeping up your practice.

Lessons 4

In part your vision will be molded by your unique life circumstances, by your personal beliefs and values. Another part will develop from your experience of the meditation practice itself, from **letting everything become your teacher**: your body, your attitudes, your mind, your pain, your joy, other people, your mistakes, your failures, your successes, nature—in short, all your moments. If you are cultivating mindfulness in your life, there is not one thing that you do or experience that cannot teach you about yourself by mirroring back to you the reflections of your own mind and body.

5 Lifelong Commitment

A s with meditation practice itself, this learning requires
a lifelong commitment to continual inquiry and a
willingness to modify your perspective as you acquire
new knowledge and arrive at new levels of
understanding and insight.

Do-It-Yourself 6

I n this regard, cultivating mindfulness is not unlike the process of eating. It would be absurd to propose that someone else eat for you. And when you go to a restaurant, you don't eat the menu, mistaking it for the meal, nor are you nourished by listening to the waiter describe the food. You have to actually eat the food for it to nourish you. In the same way, you have to **actually** *practice* mindfulness in order to reap its benefits and come to understand why it is so valuable.

- non-judging
- patience
- beginner's mind
- trust
- non-striving
- acceptance
- letting go

—seven major pillars of mindfulness practice

Right Attitude 7

The **attitude** with which you undertake the practice of paying attention and being in the present is **crucial**. It is the soil in which you will be cultivating your ability to calm your mind and to relax your body, to concentrate and to see more clearly. If the attitudinal soil is depleted, that is, if your energy and commitment to practice are low, it will be hard to develop calmness

LETTING EVERYTHING BECOME YOUR TEACHER

and relaxation with any consistency. If the soil is really polluted, that is, if you are trying to force yourself to feel relaxed and demand of yourself that "something happen," nothing will grow at all and you will quickly conclude that "meditation doesn't work."

Whole Being 8

To cultivate the healing power of mindfulness requires much more than mechanically following a recipe or a set of instructions. No real process of learning is like that. It is only when the **mind is open** and **receptive** that learning and seeing and change can occur. In practicing mindfulness you will have to bring your whole being to the process.

LETTING EVERYTHING BECOME YOUR TEACHER

9 Fresh Mind

To cultivate meditative awareness requires an entirely new way of looking at the process of learning. Since thinking that we know what we need and where we want to get is so ingrained in our minds, we can easily get caught up in trying to control things to make them turn out "our way," the way we want them to. But this attitude is antithetical to the work of awareness and healing.

Healing & Curing 10

Healing does not mean *curing*, although the two words are often used interchangeably. While it may not be possible for us to *cure* ourselves or to find someone who can, it is always possible for us to heal ourselves. *Healing* implies the possibility for us to **relate differently** to illness, disability, even death, as we learn to see with eyes of wholeness. Healing is coming to terms with things as they are.

11 Paying Attention

Awareness requires only that we pay attention and see things as they are. It doesn't require that we change anything. And healing requires receptivity and acceptance, a tuning to connectedness and wholeness. None of this can be forced, just as you cannot force yourself to go to sleep. You have to create the right conditions for falling asleep and then you have to let go. The same is true for mindfulness. It cannot be developed through force of will and striving. That kind of effort will only produce tension and frustration.

Mind-Set 12

On the other hand, if you come to the meditation practice thinking to yourself, "This won't work but I'll do it anyway," the chances are it **will not** be very helpful. The first time you feel any pain or discomfort, you will be able to say to yourself, "See, I knew my pain wouldn't go away," or "I knew I wouldn't be able to concentrate," and that will confirm your suspicion that it wasn't going to work and you will drop it.

13 How Judgmental We Are

Mindfulness is cultivated by assuming the stance of an impartial witness to your own experience. To do this requires that you become aware of the constant stream of judging and reacting to inner and outer experiences that we are all normally caught up in, and **learn to step back from it**. When we begin practicing paying attention to the activity of our own mind, it is common to discover and to be surprised by the fact that we are constantly generating judgments about our experience.

The habit of categorizing and judging our experience locks us into mechanical reactions.

14 Habitual Trap

This habit of categorizing and judging our experience locks us into **mechanical reactions** that we are not even aware of and that often have no objective basis at all. These judgments tend to dominate our minds, making it difficult for us ever to find any peace within ourselves. It's as if the mind were a yo-yo, going up and down on the string of our own judging thoughts all day long.

Clear Awareness 15

If we are to find a more effective way of handling the stress in our lives, the first thing we will need to do is to be aware of these automatic judgments so that we can **see through** our own prejudices and fears and **liberate** ourselves from their tyranny.

16 Impartial Witness

When practicing mindfulness, it is important to recognize this judging quality of mind when it appears and to **intentionally assume the stance of an impartial witness** by reminding yourself to just observe it. As Yogi Berra put it, "You can observe a lot by just watching."

Non-Judging 17

When you find the mind judging, you don't have to stop it from doing that. All that is required is to be aware of it happening. No need to judge the judging and make matters even more complicated for yourself.

18 Recognition

"This is boring," or "This isn't working," or "I can't do this." These are judgments. Actually they are just thoughts. When they come up in your mind, it is very important to **recognize** them as judgmental thinking and **remind yourself that the practice involves suspending judgment** and just watching whatever comes up, including your own judging thoughts, without pursuing them or acting on them in any way.

Natural Unfoldment 19

P atience is a form of wisdom. It demonstrates that we understand and accept the fact that sometimes things must unfold in their own time. A child may try to help a butterfly to emerge by breaking open its chrysalis. Usually the butterfly doesn't benefit from this. Any adult knows that the butterfly can emerge only in its own time, that the process cannot be hurried.

20 Self-Reminder

I n the same way we cultivate patience toward our own minds and bodies when practicing mindfulness. We **intentionally remind** ourselves that there is no need to be impatient with ourselves because we find the mind judging all the time, or because we are tense or agitated or frightened, or because we have been practicing for some time and nothing positive seems to have happened.

Each Moment Its Own 21

When such thoughts come up, they are our reality, they are part of our life unfolding in this moment. So we treat ourselves as well as we would treat the butterfly. Why rush through some moments to get to other, "better" ones? After all, each one is your life in that moment.

Mindfulness is cultivated by
assuming the stance of an
impartial witness to your own
experience.

Not Being Present 22

One of the mind's favorite activities is to wander into the past and into the future and lose itself in thinking. Some of its thoughts are pleasant. Others are painful and anxiety producing. In either case thinking itself **exerts a strong pull** on our awareness. Much of the time our thoughts overwhelm our perception of the present moment. They cause us to lose our connection to the present.

Acceptance

Patience can be a particularly helpful quality to invoke when the mind is agitated. It can help us to accept this wandering tendency of the mind while reminding us that we don't have to get caught up in its travels. Practicing patience reminds us that we don't have to fill up our moments with activity and with more thinking in order for them to be rich. In fact it helps us to remember that quite the opposite is true. To be patient is simply to be completely open to each moment, accepting it in its fullness, knowing that, like the butterfly, things can unfold only in their own time.

Beginner's Mind 24

The richness of present-moment experience is the richness of life itself. Too often we let our thinking and our beliefs about what we "know" prevent us from seeing things as they really are. We tend to take the ordinary for granted and fail to grasp the extraordinariness of the ordinary. To see the richness of the present moment, we need to cultivate what has been called "beginner's mind," a mind that is willing to see everything as if for the first time.

25 Receptiveness

An open, "beginner's" mind allows us to be receptive to new possibilities and prevents us from getting stuck in the rut of our own expertise, which often thinks it knows more than it does.

Seeing Afresh 26

No moment is the same as any other. Each is unique and contains unique possibilities. Beginner's mind reminds us of this simple truth. The next time you see somebody who is familiar to you, ask yourself if you are seeing this person with fresh eyes, as he or she really is, or if you are seeing only the reflection of your own thoughts about this person.

Uncluttered Mind

Try it when you are outdoors in nature. Are you able to see the sky, the stars, the trees and the water and the stones, and really see them as they are right now with a clear and uncluttered mind? Or are you actually seeing them only through the veil of your own thoughts and opinions?

Live Our Own Life 28

It is impossible to become like somebody else. Your only hope is to become **more fully yourself**. That is the reason for practicing meditation in the first place. Teachers and books and CDs can only be guides, signposts. It is important to be open and receptive to what you can learn from other sources, but ultimately you still have to live your own life, every moment of it.

29 Trust

In practicing mindfulness, you are practicing taking responsibility for being yourself and learning to listen to and trust your own being. The more you cultivate this trust in your own being, the easier you will find it will be to trust other people more and to see their basic goodness as well.

Just keep practicing.

30 Self-Discipline

Mindfulness doesn't just come about by itself because you have decided that it is a good idea to be more aware of things in the present moment, and less judgmental. Mindfulness is not merely a good idea. A **strong commitment** to nurturing yourself and mustering enough self-discipline to persevere in the process is essential to developing a strong meditation practice and a high degree of mindfulness. **Self-discipline and regular practice** are vital to developing the power of mindfulness.

Commitment 31

The spirit of engaged commitment to meditation is similar to that required in athletic training. The athlete who is training for a particular event doesn't practice only when he or she feels like it, for instance, only when the weather is nice or there are other people to keep him or her company or there is enough time to fit it in. The athlete **trains regularly**, every day, rain or shine, whether she feels good or not, whether the goal seems worth it or not on any particular day.

32 Just Do It

You don't have to like it; you just have to do it.

Making Time 33

Our lives are so complex and our minds so busy and agitated most of the time that it is necessary, especially at the beginning, to protect and support your meditation practice by making a special time for it and, if possible, by making a special place in your home where you will feel particularly comfortable and "at home" while practicing. Just making this amount of time every day for yourself will be a very positive lifestyle change and gift to yourself.

34 Creating Conditions

This time for formal meditation practice needs to be protected from interruptions and from other commitments so that you can just be yourself without having to do or respond to anything. This is not always possible, but it is helpful if you can manage to set things up in this way.

Letting Go 35

O ne measure of your commitment is whether you can bring yourself to shut off your telephones for the time you will be practicing and let them take messages. It is a **great letting go** in and of itself only to be home for yourself at those times, and great peace can follow from this alone.

36 Keeping to the Path

O nce you make the commitment to yourself to practice in this way, the self-discipline comes in carrying it out. Committing yourself to goals that are in your own self-interest is easy. But keeping to the path you have chosen when you run into obstacles and may not see "results" right away is the real measure of your commitment.

Conscious Intention 37

This is where **conscious intentionality** comes in, the intention to practice whether you feel like it or not on a particular day, whether it is convenient or not, with the determination of an athlete, but for its own sake, because this moment is your life.

Mindfulness doesn't just
come about by itself.

Regular Practice 38

Regular practice is not as hard as you might think once you make up your mind to do it and pick an appropriate time. Most people are inwardly disciplined already to a certain extent. Getting dinner on the table every night requires discipline. Getting up in the morning and going to work requires discipline. And taking time for yourself certainly does too.

39 Reason for Committing

Perhaps the ability to function more effectively under pressure or to be healthier and to feel better, or to be more relaxed and self-confident and happy, will suffice as reasons to take up meditation seriously. Ultimately you have to decide for yourself why you are making such a commitment.

Self-Deception 40

Some people have resistance to the whole idea of taking time for themselves. Some people discover that they have a little voice inside that tells them that it is selfish or that they are undeserving of this kind of time and energy. Usually they recognize it as a message they were given very early on in their lives: "Live for others, not for yourself." "Help others; don't dwell on yourself."

If you do feel undeserving of taking time for yourself, why not **look at** *that* as part of your mindfulness practice? Where do such feelings come from? What are the thoughts behind them? Can you observe them with acceptance? Are they accurate?

Intelligent 42

Even the degree to which you can really be of help to others, if that is what you believe is most important, depends directly on how balanced you are yourself. Taking time to "tune" your own instrument and restore your energy reserves can hardly be considered selfish. *Intelligent* would be a more apt description.

LETTING EVERYTHING BECOME YOUR TEACHER

Happily, once people start practicing mindfulness, most quickly get over the idea that it is "selfish" and "narcissistic" to take time for themselves as they see the difference that making some time to just be has on the quality of their lives and their self-esteem, as well as on their relationships.

Being Awake 44

If I feel groggy when I wake up in the morning, I might splash cold water on my face until I know I am really awake. I don't want to meditate in a daze. I want to be alert. This may seem somewhat extreme, but really it is just knowing the **value of being awake** before trying to practice.

Pay attention.
Nothing more.

Wakefulness 45

It helps to remember that mindfulness is about being fully awake. It is not cultivated by relaxing to the point where unawareness and sleep take over. So we advocate doing anything necessary to wake up, even taking a cold shower if that is what it takes.

Dispelling the Fog

Your **meditation practice** will only be as powerful as your motivation to dispel the fog of your own lack of awareness. When you are in this fog, it is hard to remember the importance of practicing mindfulness, and it is hard to locate your attitudinal bearings. Confusion, fatigue, depression, and anxiety are powerful mental states that can undermine your best intentions to practice regularly. You can easily get caught up and then stuck in them and not even know it.

Stability & Resilience

That is when your commitment to practice is of greatest value. It keeps you engaged in the process. The momentum of regular practice helps to maintain a certain mental stability and resilience even as you go through states of turmoil, confusion, lack of clarity, and procrastination.

48 A Refuge

To get back in touch with being is not that difficult. We only need to remind ourselves to be mindful. Moments of mindfulness are moments of peace and stillness, even in the midst of activity. When your whole life is driven by doing, formal meditation practice can provide a refuge of sanity and stability that can be used to restore some balance and perspective. It can be a way of stopping the headlong momentum of all the doing and giving yourself some time to dwell in a state of deep relaxation and well-being and to remember who you are.

Strength 49

The formal practice can give you the strength and the self-knowledge to go back to the doing and do it from out of your being. Then at least a certain amount of patience and inner stillness, clarity, and balance of mind will infuse what you are doing, and the busyness and pressure will be less onerous. In fact they might just disappear entirely.

50 Non-Doing

Meditation is really a non-doing. It is the only human endeavor I know of that does not involve trying to get somewhere else but, rather, emphasizes **being where you already are**. Much of the time we are so carried away by all the doing, the striving, the planning, the reacting, the busyness, that when we stop just to feel where we are, it can seem a little peculiar at first.

Stop & Observe 51

For one thing, we tend to have little awareness of the incessant and relentless activity of our own mind and how much we are driven by it. That is not too surprising, given that we hardly ever stop and observe the mind directly to see what it is up to.

52 Out of Control

I ronically, although we all "have" minds, we seem to need to "re-mind" ourselves of who we are from time to time. If we don't, the momentum of all the doing just takes over and can have us living its agenda rather than our own, almost as if we were robots.

Mind*fulness*.
Mind*lessness*.

53 Unknowing

The momentum of unbridled doing can carry us for decades, even to the grave, **without our quite knowing** that we are living out our lives and that we have only moments to live.

Re-minding 54

G iven all the momentum behind our doing, getting ourselves to remember the preciousness of the present moment seems to require somewhat unusual and even drastic steps. This is why we **make a special time** each day for formal meditation practice. It is a way of stopping, a way of "re-minding" ourselves, of nourishing the domain of being for a change. It's a way of "re-bodying" too.

55 Just Observe

In practicing meditation, we don't try to answer questions.
Rather we **just observe** the impulse to get up from
the sitting, or to get caught in the thoughts
that come into the mind.

Basic Instruction 56

Each time we become aware that the mind is off someplace else . . . that it has forgotten the present, we first note what is actually on our mind in that moment, whatever it is, and then we **gently bring our attention back** to our abdomen, back to the sensation of the rising and falling of our belly, no matter what carried it away. If the attention moves off the breath a hundred times, then we just **calmly bring it back** a hundred times, as soon as we are aware of not being in the present and where our mind has alighted.

57 Momentary Importance

By practicing in this way, you are training your mind to be less reactive and more stable. You are **making each moment** count. You are taking each moment as it comes, not valuing any one above any other. In this way you are cultivating your natural ability to concentrate and calm your own mind.

Mental Muscles 58

By repeatedly bringing your attention back to the breath each time it wanders off, concentration builds and deepens, much as muscles develop by repetitively lifting weights. And by repeatedly noting, without reaction, what is on your mind when it is carried off, you are developing greater awareness of the mind itself and insight into how self-distracting and emotionally turbulent it can be.

Experiment mindfully!
Find out
what works
for you.

Potentials 59

Attending to experience in this way, any pain in your knee that might arise with time, or aching in your back, or tension in your shoulders, rather than being treated as distractions preventing you from staying with your breath, can be included in the field of your awareness and simply accepted without reacting to them as undesirable and trying to make them go away. This approach gives you an alternate way of seeing discomfort.

Uncomfortable as they may be, these bodily sensations are now **potential teachers** and **allies** in learning about yourself. They can help you to develop your powers of concentration, calmness, and awareness rather than just being frustrating impediments to the goal of trying to stay on your breath.

Inner Strength 60

Working regularly with (not struggling against) the resistance of your mind builds **inner strength**. At the same time you are also developing patience and practicing being non-judgmental.

Flexibility

The cultivation of this kind of flexibility, which allows you to welcome *whatever* comes up and be with it rather than insisting on paying attention to only one thing, say the breath, is one of the most characteristic and valuable features of mindfulness meditation.

Non-Reaction 62

What this means in practice is that we make some effort to sit *with* sensations of discomfort when they come up during our attempts to meditate, not necessarily to the point of pain but at least past where we might ordinarily react to them. We **welcome them** and actually try to maintain a continuity of awareness from moment to moment in their presence. Then, if we have to, we shift our body to reduce the discomfort, but *we do even that mindfully*, with moment-to-moment awareness as we are moving.

Relaxing into discomfort reduces pain intensity.

Thinking Is Not Bad 63

Letting go of our thoughts, however, does not mean
suppressing them. Many people hear it this way and
make the mistake of thinking that meditation requires them to
shut off their thinking or their feelings. They somehow hear the
instructions as meaning that if they are thinking, that is "bad,"
and that a "good meditation" is one in which there is little or no
thinking. So it is important to emphasize that thinking is not bad

nor is it even undesirable during meditation. What matters is whether you are aware of your thoughts and feelings during meditation and how you handle them. Trying to suppress them will only result in greater tension and frustration and more problems, not in calmness and peace.

Letting Be 64

Mindfulness does not involve pushing thoughts away or walling yourself off from them to quiet your mind. We are not trying to stop our thoughts as they cascade through the mind. We are simply **making room for them**, observing them as thoughts, and letting them be, using the breath as our anchor or "home base" for observing, for reminding us to stay focused and calm.

65 Making Room

Meditation is not so concerned with how much thinking is going on as it is with how much room you are making for it to take place within the field of your awareness from one moment to the next.

Being Attentive 66

If the thought of how much you have to get done today comes up while you are meditating, you will have to be very attentive to it *as a thought* or you may be up and doing things before you know it, without any awareness that you decided to stop sitting simply because a thought came through your mind.

67 Power of Recognition

On the other hand, when such a thought comes up, if you are able to step back from it and see it clearly, then you will be able to prioritize things and make sensible decisions about what really does need doing. You will know when to call it quits during the day. So the simple act of recognizing your thoughts *as thoughts* can free you from the distorted reality they often create and allow for more clear-sightedness and a greater sense of manageability in your life.

Liberation from Tyranny 68

This **liberation** from the tyranny of the thinking mind comes directly out of the meditation practice itself. When we spend some time each day in a state of non-doing, observing the flow of the breath and the activity of our mind and body without getting caught up in that activity, we are cultivating calmness and mindfulness hand in hand.

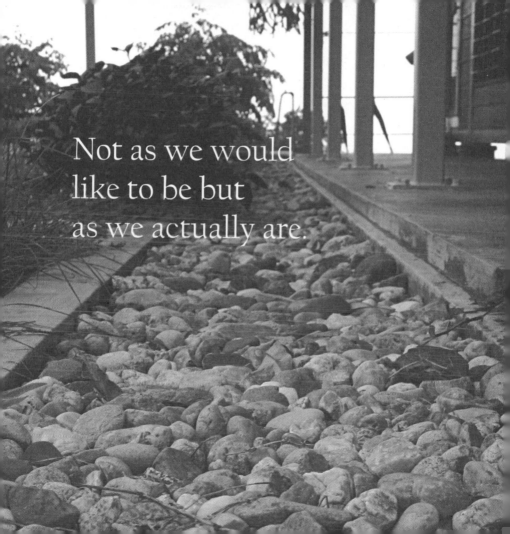

Not as we would
like to be but
as we actually are.

Knowing Ourselves

As the mind develops stability and is less caught up in the content of thinking, we strengthen the mind's ability to concentrate and to be calm. And each time we recognize a thought as a thought when it arises, and we register its content and discern the strength of its hold on us and the accuracy of its content, each time we then let go of it and come back to our breathing and to a sense of our body, we are strengthening mindfulness. We are coming to know ourselves better and becoming more accepting of ourselves, not as we would like to be but as we actually are.

LETTING EVERYTHING BECOME YOUR TEACHER

70 Getting Nowhere

Our patients come to the stress reduction clinic hoping to have something positive happen, yet we advise them to practice **without trying to get anywhere**. Instead, we encourage them to try to be fully where they already are, with acceptance. In addition, we suggest they suspend judgment for the eight weeks that they are in the course and decide only at the end whether it was worthwhile.

Starting from Scratch 71

Why do we take this approach? Creating this paradoxical situation invites people to explore non-striving and self-acceptance as ways of being. It gives them permission to start from scratch, to tap a new way of seeing and feeling **without holding up** standards of success and failure based on a habitual and limited way of seeing their problems and their expectations about what they should be feeling.

We practice the meditation in this way because the effort to try to "get somewhere" is so often the wrong kind of effort for catalyzing change or growth or healing, coming as it usually does from a rejection of present-moment reality without having a full awareness and understanding of that reality.

Wishful Thinking 72

A desire for things to be other than the way they actually are is simply **wishful thinking**. It is not a very effective way of bringing about real change. At the first signs of what you think is "failure," when you see that you are not "getting anywhere" or have not gotten where you thought you should be, you are likely to get discouraged or feel overwhelmed, lose hope, blame external forces, and give up.

73 Accepting the Present

The meditative view is that it is only through the **acceptance** of the **actuality of the present**, no matter how painful or frightening or undesirable it may be, change and growth and healing can come about. They need only be nurtured in order to unfold and be *dis-covered*.

Nowhere Else to Go   74

Y ou only need to really be where you already are and *realize* it (make it real). In fact, in this way of looking at things *there is no place else to go*, so efforts to get anywhere else are ill-conceived. They are bound to lead to frustration and failure. On the other hand, you cannot fail to be where you already are. So you cannot "fail" in your meditation practice if you are willing to be with things as they are.

Change: one thing
you can be sure of.

Beyond Success & Failure

In its truest expression, meditation goes beyond notions of success and failure, and this is why it is such a powerful vehicle for growth and change and healing. This does not mean that you cannot progress in your meditation practice, nor does it mean that it is impossible to make mistakes that will reduce its value to you. A particular kind of effort *is* necessary in the practice of meditation, but it is not an effort of striving to achieve some special state, whether it be relaxation, freedom from pain, healing, or insight. These come naturally with practice because they are already inherent in the present moment and in every moment. Therefore any moment is as good as any other for experiencing their presence within yourself.

If you see things in this light, it makes perfect sense to take each moment as it comes and accept it as it is, seeing it clearly in its fullness, and letting it go.

When you feel connected
to something, that
connection immediately
gives you a purpose for
living.

Honoring
Each Moment 77

I f you are unsure of whether you are practicing "correctly" or
not, here is a good litmus test: When you notice thoughts in
the mind about getting somewhere, about wanting something,
or about having gotten somewhere, about "success" or "failure,"
are you able to honor each one as you observe it as
an aspect of present-moment reality? Can you see it

clearly as an impulse, a thought, a desire, a judgment, and
let it be here and let it go without being drawn into it,
without investing it with a power it doesn't have, without
losing yourself in the process?
This is the way to cultivate mindfulness.

One simple way of bringing awareness into your daily life is to practice walking meditation. As you might guess, this means bringing your attention to the actual experience of walking as you are doing it. It means simply walking *and knowing* that you are walking. It does *not* mean looking at your feet! One of the things that you find out when you have been practicing mindfulness for a while is that nothing is quite as simple as it appears. This is as true for walking as it is for anything else. For one thing, we carry our mind with us when we walk, so we are usually absorbed in our own thoughts to one extent or another. We are hardly ever just walking, even when we are "just going for a walk."

Internal Observation 79

We begin by making an effort to be **fully aware** as one foot contacts the ground, as the weight shifts to it, as the other foot lifts and moves ahead and then comes down to make contact with the ground in its turn. As with all the other methods we have been exploring, when the mind wanders away from the feet or the legs or the feeling of the body walking, we simply bring it back when we become aware of it. To deepen our concentration, we do not look around at the sights but keep our gaze focused in front of us. We also don't look at our feet. They know how to walk quite well on their own. It is an internal observation that is being cultivated, just the felt sensations of walking, nothing more.

Dynamism in Walking 80

Because we tend to live so unconsciously, we take things like the ability to walk very much for granted. When you start paying more attention to it, you will **appreciate** that it is an amazing balancing act, given the small surface area of our two feet. It took us about a year as a baby to be ready to learn this dynamic balancing act of locomotion.

The Great Wonder of Walking

On any given day in the hospital there are many people who are unable to walk because of injury or illness, and some who will never walk again. For all these people, just being able to take one step unassisted—no less walk down the hall or out to a car—is a miracle. Yet we hardly ever appreciate the great wonder of walking. When we practice walking meditation, we are not trying to get anywhere. It is sufficient to just be with each step, realizing that you are just where you are. **The trick is to be there completely**, and then it is no longer *there*—but *here*.

Do not try stopping or pushing thoughts away. Make room for them, observing them as thoughts, and letting them be.

Fullness 82

There are probably circumstances of one kind or another in your life in which you have to be walking, whether you like it or not. These can be wonderful occasions to bring awareness to your walking and thereby transform it from a dull, mostly unconscious chore into something rich and nurturing.

83 Life Blessings

Everything our body normally does is quite wonderful and extraordinary, though you may hardly ever think of it this way. Walking is a good example. If you have ever been unable to walk, you will know how **precious** and **miraculous** walking is. It is an extraordinary capability. So are seeing and talking, thinking and breathing, being able to turn over in bed, and anything else you choose to focus on that your body does.

Gentling Yourself 84

Mindfulness practice is playful, but it is also hard work, and there will be times when you will feel like quitting, especially if you have a chronic pain condition and don't see quick "results" in terms of pain reduction. In doing this work, it is very helpful to remember that it asks for patience and gentleness and lovingkindness toward yourself and even toward your pain. It means working at your limits, but gently, not trying too hard, not exhausting yourself, not pushing too hard to break through.

The breakthroughs will come by themselves in their own good time if you put in the energy in the spirit of self-discovery. Mindfulness does not bulldoze through resistance. You have to work gently at the edges, a little here and a little there, keeping your vision alive in your heart, particularly during the times of greatest pain and difficulty.

Consistency 85

Regular practice is necessary, as we have been stressing all along. The domain of being is easier to talk about than to experience. To make it real in your life, to get in touch with it in any moment, takes concentrated work and determination. A certain kind of digging, a kind of inner archaeology, is required to uncover your intrinsic wholeness, covered over as it may be with layer after layer of opinions, likes and dislikes,

and the heavy fog of automatic, unconscious thinking and habits,
to say nothing of pain. There is nothing romantic or sentimental
about the work of mindfulness, nor is your intrinsic wholeness
a romantic or sentimental or imaginary construct. It is
here now, as it always has been. It is part of being human,
just as having a body and feeling pain are part of being human.

Relating to Sensation 86

If you try to bring mindfulness to exactly what you are feeling in those moments when you hurt yourself accidentally, you will probably find that how you relate to the sensations you experience makes a big difference in the degree of pain you actually feel and how much you suffer.

87 Pain & Suffering

Aversion to pain is really a misplaced aversion to suffering. Ordinarily we do not make a distinction between pain and suffering, but there are very important differences between them. Pain is a natural part of the experience of life. Suffering is one of many possible responses to pain. Suffering can come out of either physical or emotional pain. It involves our thoughts and emotions and how they frame the meaning of our experiences. **Suffering, too, is perfectly natural.** In fact the human condition is often spoken of as inevitable suffering. However, it may be more accurate to say that while pain is inevitable, suffering is optional.

Your pain is not you.

Pain as Response 88

I t is important to remember that suffering is only *one*
response to the experience of pain. Even a small pain can
produce great suffering in us if we fear that it means we have a
tumor or some other frightening condition. That same pain can
be seen as nothing at all, a minor ache or inconvenience, once
we are reassured that all the tests are negative and there is no
chance that it is a sign of something serious. So it is not always
the pain per se but the way we see it and react to it
that determines the degree of suffering we will experience.
And it is the suffering that we fear most, not the pain.

LETTING EVERYTHING BECOME YOUR TEACHER

In fact, even if distraction does alleviate your pain or help you to cope with it some of the time, bringing mindfulness to it can lead to new levels of insight and understanding about yourself and your body, which distraction or escape can never do. Understanding and insight, of course, are an extremely important part of the process of coming to terms with your condition and really learning *how* to live with it, not just endure it.

Tuning in to Pain 90

Some people have difficulty understanding why we emphasize that they try to enter *into* their pain when they simply hate it and just want it to go away. Their feeling is "Why shouldn't I just ignore it or distract myself from it and grit my teeth and just endure it when it is too great?" One reason is that there may be times when ignoring it or distracting yourself doesn't work. At such times, it is very helpful to have other tricks up your sleeve besides just trying to endure it or depending on drugs to ease it. Several laboratory experiments with acute pain have shown that *tuning in* to sensations is a more effective way of reducing the level of pain experienced when the pain is intense and prolonged than is distracting yourself.

A Matter of Choice 91

If you have a chronic pain condition, or for that matter, any chronic problem with your body or mind, you will be more aware than anybody that having pain doesn't free you from all the other kinds of problems and difficulties people have. Your other life problems need to be faced too. You can work with them in the same way you will face and work with pain. It is important to remind yourself, especially if you feel discouraged and depressed at times, that you still have the ability to feel joy and pleasure in your life, and that they may actually be present right now. If you remember to **cultivate this wider view** of yourself, your efforts in the meditation will have a much more fertile soil in which to produce positive results. The meditation may also wind up helping you in unsuspected ways having nothing to do with your pain.

It is not helpful to *expect* pain to disappear. But you may find that it changes in intensity, getting momentarily stronger or weaker, or that the sensations change, say from sharp to dull, or to tingling or burning or throbbing. It can also be helpful to be aware of any thoughts and emotional reactions that you may be having about the pain, your body, the meditation, or anything else. Just keep up the watching and letting go, watching and letting go, breath by breath, moment by moment.

93 Being with the Present

The key to approaching pain is your unwavering determination to direct your attention gently, delicately, but firmly *on* and *into* the pain, no matter how bad it seems. After all, it is what you are feeling right now, so you might as well see if you can befriend it a little bit at least, just because it is here.

Healing Takes Time 94

Do not be overly thrilled with "success" or overly depressed by lack of "progress" as you go along. **Every day will be different.** In fact every moment will be different, so don't jump to conclusions after one or two sessions. The work of growth and healing takes time. It requires **patience** and **consistency** in the meditation practice over a period of weeks, if not months and years.

If you have had a problem with pain for a number of years, it is not exactly reasonable to expect that it will magically go away in a matter of days just because you have started to meditate. But, especially if you have tried everything else already and still have pain, what do you have to lose by practicing the meditation on a regular basis for a period of time, or even longer?

This adventure has all the elements of a heroic quest, a search for yourself along the path of life.

Non-Confrontation

In some moments when you go into your pain and face it openly, it may seem as if you are locked in hand-to-hand combat with it or as if you are undergoing torture. It is helpful to recognize that these are just thoughts. It helps to remind yourself that the work of mindfulness is *not* meant to be a battle between you and your pain and it won't be unless you make it into one. If you do make it a struggle, it will only make for greater tension and therefore more pain.

Mindfulness involves a determined **effort to observe and accept** your physical discomfort and your agitated emotions, moment by moment.

R emember, you are **trying to find out** about your pain, to learn from it, to know it better, not to stop it or get rid of it or escape from it.

98 Being with Pain

I f you can assume this attitude and be calmly *with* your pain, looking at it in this way for even one breath or even half a breath, that is a step in the right direction. From there you might be able to expand it and remain calm and open while facing the pain for maybe two or three breaths or even longer.

The way of awareness is
always here, always
accessible to you,
in each moment.

99 Riding with It

Since pain is already present in a particular moment, we do what we can to be receptive and accepting of it. We try to relate to it in as neutral a way as possible, observing it non-judgmentally, feeling what it actually feels like in detail. This involves opening up to the raw sensations themselves, whatever they may be. We breathe with them and dwell with them from moment to moment, riding the waves of the breath, the waves of sensation.

Fully Present 100

We can ask ourselves the question "How bad is it right now, in this very moment?" If you practice in this way, you will probably find that most of the time, even when you are feeling terrible, when you go right into the sensations and ask, "IN THIS MOMENT, is it tolerable? Is it okay?" the chances are you will find that it is. The difficulty is that the next moment is coming, and the next, and you "*know*" they are all going to be filled with more pain. The solution? Try taking each moment as it comes. Try to be one hundred percent *in* the present in one moment, then do the same for the next.

You have only moments to live.

LETTING EVERYTHING BECOME YOUR TEACHER
A Delta Book / May 2009
Excerpts from *Full Catastrophe Living*

Published by
Bantam Dell
A Division of Random House, Inc.
New York, New York

Layout, design, and photography by Hor Tuck Loon
Cover photograph by Wunson/Shutterstock
Cover design and image manipulation by Beverly Leung

Delta is a registered trademark of Random House, Inc.,
and the colophon is a trademark of Random House, Inc.

Library of Congress Cataloging-in-Publication Data
Kabat-Zinn, Jon.
Letting everything become your teacher: 100 lessons in mindfulness /
Jon Kabat-Zinn; excerpts from Full catastrophe living compiled by Hor Tuck Loon and Jon Kabat-Zinn.
p. cm.
ISBN 978-0-385-34323-7 (trade pbk.)
1. Meditation. 2. Attention. 3. Stress management. 4. Stress
(Psychology) I. Hor, Tuck Loon. II. Kabat-Zinn, Jon. Full catastrophe living. Selections. III. Title.
BF637.M4K225 2009 158.1—dc22 2008055234

Printed in the United States of America
Published simultaneously in Canada

www.bantamdell.com

ROS 1 0 9 8 7 6